CAST IRON COOKBOOK

Timeless One-Pot Recipes
for Everyday
Cooking or Special Occasions

CHRISTOPHER LESTER

Table of Contents

INTRODUCTION

Get ready, as we're about to embark on a wild culinary journey far beyond the usual pots and pans! Prepare to discover the magical wonders of cast-iron cookware and reveal a world of endless deliciousness.

Cast iron is not your typical cookware. On the contrary, it's a universal wizard that can turn your dishes into true masterpieces, whether you're a seasoned professional or a novice cook.

Cast iron cookware has a long history. Its incredible durability and ability to evenly distribute heat and hold it securely have made it a cherished treasure among respected chefs and home cooking heroes. Using cast iron, you will not only create admirable dishes but also bring nostalgia to your culinary adventures.

Just imagine the sizzle of a perfectly grilled steak, its succulent tenderness captivating your taste buds. Imagine the heavenly aroma of freshly baked cornbread, its golden crust whispering promises of delight. Nor should you overlook the mouthwatering wonders of an aromatic stew slowly simmering and filling your humble abode with an intoxicating symphony of smells. These tantalizing dreams can become your daily reality thanks to the mystical power of cast iron. Get ready for an unparalleled restaurant-quality experience in the cozy embrace of your kitchen.

So, dear lovers of culinary adventure, are you ready to step into the enchanting realm of cast iron cookware? All aspiring cast-iron wizards and kitchen adventurers are welcome! Are you ready to discover the secret spells and alluring tricks of cooking in cast iron? Well, you're in luck because the magical Cast Iron Cookbook will tell you all the secrets!

We'll arm you with the essential knowledge of basic cooking techniques that will make you a true cast iron maestro. But that's not all, dear culinary wizard! We've also assembled a treasure trove of mouthwatering recipes to fire up your taste buds and mesmerize your loved ones.

So put on your favorite apron, polish your cast iron skillet, and together, we'll conquer uncharted flavor territories, unleash your inner culinary creativity, and create dishes that will have your family and friends begging for more.

Gather your culinary courage, grab your chopstick (or spatula), and let's go on a culinary adventure. It's time to master the art of cooking in cast iron and take your kitchen wizardry to extraordinary heights. The kingdom of taste awaits you!

A BRIEF HISTORY OF CAST IRON COOKING

The history of cooking with cast iron goes back thousands of years. The earliest cast iron artifacts date back to ancient China, around the 5th century BC. By the 18th and 19th centuries, however, cast iron cookware had become widespread and a staple in many culinary cultures.

The invention of sand-casting technology enabled the mass production of cast iron cookware. Cast iron cookware became more accessible to more people.

In the United States, cast iron cookware became especially popular in the 19th century. Cast iron pans, Dutch ovens, and grills were indispensable tools for the early homesteaders as they settled new territories. Improvements in manufacturing technology led to smoother surfaces and lighter-weight cast iron pans. However, with the advent of modern non-stick coatings, cast iron fell out of use for a time.

Lately, there has been a renewed fascination in the art of cooking using cast iron. People have rediscovered the many benefits of cooking in cast iron, such as heat retention and distribution, as well as durability. Cast iron cookware has also come in handy for outdoor and grilling enthusiasts.

Chefs appreciate cast iron cookware for its versatility. It can be used with stoves, ovens, grills, and even campfires. You can cook almost anything in it — from grilling steaks to baking bread and stewing juicy meats.

The rich history of cast iron cookware has made it an iconic and timeless choice for professional chefs and home cooks alike. Its longevity and exceptional culinary capabilities ensure that cast iron cookware will continue to be cherished and passed down from generation to generation.

THE WORLDWIDE POPULARITY OF CAST IRON COOKING

Cast iron cookware is a great helper in the kitchen. It has conquered the culinary world thanks to its indispensable key properties:

- **Durability:** It withstands high temperatures and is resistant to chipping, cracking, and warping. With proper care, cast iron pots and pans can last for generations, making them a great investment.

- **Heat retention:** Cast iron heats slowly and evenly, distributing heat over the entire cooking surface. This makes it ideal for frying, roasting, and maintaining a consistent temperature while cooking.

- **Versatility:** Cast iron cookware can be utilized with various heat sources such as stovetop, oven, grill, and even over an open fire. You can fry, sauté, bake, roast, and even braise in it. The ability to transition smoothly from stove to oven is embraced by professional cooks and home cooks alike.

- **Non-stick properties:** A well-seasoned cast iron skillet acquires a natural non-stick surface over time. The seasoning is formed by the oil bonding with the cast iron, forming a smooth coating that keeps food from sticking. This makes cast iron very convenient for cooking delicate dishes such as eggs and fish.

- **Health benefits:** Cooking with cast iron can have health benefits, too. A small amount of iron naturally enters the food during cooking, which can benefit people who are iron deficient. In addition, because cast iron has no non-stick coating that can release harmful chemicals, it is considered a safe and non-toxic option for cooking.

- **Traditional and rustic appeal:** Cast iron cookware has a nostalgic and rustic charm. It is often associated with traditional recipes and home cooking, evoking a sense of heritage and authenticity. Many appreciate the connection to the past that cooking in cast iron cookware brings.

- **Eco-friendly:** Cast iron cookware is eco-friendly. It is made from recycled materials and is highly durable, reducing the need to replace cookware frequently. In addition, cast iron is easily restorable, further prolonging its lifespan.

From chefs in fancy restaurants to home cooking enthusiasts, cast iron is valued for its unmatched durability, super adaptability, and the mouthwatering magic it brings to food.

COOKING TECHNIQUES AND TIPS

PROPERTIES OF CAST IRON

Cast iron rocks the culinary world with its cool heat distribution and retention. No wonder cast iron is the hottest superstar in the kitchen! Let's dive into the sizzling details of its heat magic:

Heat Distribution:

When heated, cast iron retains and distributes heat throughout its entire structure, ensuring even cooking. This property is especially useful for stewing, roasting, and baking.

The high thermal conductivity of cast iron allows rapid heat transfer from the heat source to the cooking surface. As a result, cast iron pans provide fast and even heat distribution, eliminating hot and cold spots on the cooking surface.

Heat retention:

Cast iron can retain a significant amount of heat for long periods. Once heated, cast iron retains heat much more efficiently than stainless steel or aluminum.

This property works especially well for long, slow cooking methods or keeping food warm. Cast iron cookware can be preheated and kept at a constant temperature, ensuring even cooking for long periods. This is especially useful for dishes that require simmering or braising.

Keep in mind, however, that cast iron takes longer to heat up initially than some other materials, so preheating is often recommended for maximum heat distribution and retention.

PREHEATING AND TEMPERATURE CONTROL

Proper preheating and temperature control are crucial when using cast iron cookware to ensure the best cooking results. Catch my recommendations for trouble-free cooking:

Preheat cast iron:

Start by placing the cast iron skillet or pan on the stove over medium heat.

- Allow the skillet to heat gradually for 5 to 10 minutes. This will ensure even heating and help avoid hot spots.

- You can check the temperature by flicking a few drops of water onto the surface. If the water sizzles and evaporates almost immediately, the pan is ready to use.

- To roast meat or get a good crust on foods, preheat a cast-iron skillet over medium-high heat until it is hot.

- Preheat the cast iron over medium to medium-high heat for delicate dishes or recipes requiring less heat.

Temperature control:

- Cast iron cookware holds heat well, so reduce the heat to low after reaching your desired temperature.

- Avoid using high heat all the time, as it may cause uneven heating or burning.

- If more heat is needed, increase the heat gradually.

Additional tips:

- A cast-iron pan takes a long time to heat up, and even after you remove it from the heat, the pan will remain hot. Be careful and use appropriate oven mitts or lids with handles.

- Do not immediately place a hot cast iron skillet under cold water. This can cause it to crack or deform.

- Allow the cast iron to cool naturally after cooking before cleaning it.

- Keep in mind that specific temperatures and heating times may vary depending on the recipe you are following, so always read recipes carefully for the best results.

FRYING AND BROWNING THE MEAT

Roasting and browning meat in a cast-iron skillet is a popular cooking method that helps improve the flavor and texture of meat. So, friends, get ready to unleash your inner kitchen wizard with my proven recommendations:

1. Place the cast iron skillet over medium-high heat on the stove. Allow several minutes for the skillet to heat up until it reaches a hot temperature.

2. Wipe the meat dry so it cooks better. Rub salt, pepper, or other seasonings over the meat.

3. Add oil or fat to the hot pan. You can use vegetable oil (such as canola oil), ghee, or bacon grease.

4. Place the meat in the skillet, ensuring it makes even contact with the surface.

5. Cook the meat briefly until it achieves a desirable golden-brown color. This will help preserve the juices and enhance the flavor.

6. Flip the meat with tongs and brown the other side. The cooking time will vary based on the thickness and type of meat being prepared.

7. If the skillet gets too hot or the meat starts to burn, you can reduce the heat to medium or medium-low.

8. Use a meat thermometer or make a small cut to check the meat's internal temperature and ensure it is cooked.

9. When the meat is cooked, remove it from the skillet and let it sit for a few minutes before serving. This will redistribute the juices and provide a tender and flavorful result.

BRAISING AND SLOW COOKING

Its ability to retain heat and distribute it evenly make cast iron cookware ideal for slow cooking or braising.

Here's a general guide to braising and slow cooking in cast iron:

1. **Choose the right cut of meat:** Braising is often used for tougher cuts of meat with lots of connective tissue, such as roasts, brisket, or short ribs. These cuts benefit from a slow cooking process that breaks down collagen and makes them tender and juicy.

2. **Preheat your cast-iron pan:** Place it over medium heat and heat it for a few minutes. This will help ensure even cooking.

3. **Season and roast the meat:** Season the meat and roast until brown. Remove the roasted meat from the pan and set it aside while you complete the next step.

4. **Add aromatics and liquid:** Add chopped onions, carrots, garlic, or other aromatics to the pot and stir-fry until softened and fragrant. Pour in liquids such as broth, wine, or a combination of these to create a flavorful braising liquid.

5. **Return the meat to the pot:** Place the roasted meat back in the pot, submerging it in the braising liquid.

6. **Cover and braise:** Cover the pot with a lid and reduce the heat to low. Braise the meat over low heat for a long time, usually several hours, until tender.

7. **Check and adjust the liquid:** Periodically check the dish to ensure the braising liquid has not evaporated completely. Add more liquid as needed to maintain the proper level. You can also ladle the stewing liquid over the meat periodically to keep it moist and flavorful.

8. **Serve:** When the meat is tender, remove it from the pot and strain out the stewing liquid. The liquid can be used as a sauce. Slice the meat and serve it with the sauce and garnish of your choice.

The wonderful combination of ingredients and the magic of braising in reliable cast iron will open the door to unlimited experimentation. Imagine succulent roasts, fragrant stews, tender braised chicken, and hearty vegetable wonders. So, choose the recipe that appeals to you and pull out your cast-iron pot. Enjoy the process *and* the result!

BAKING AND ROASTING IN CAST IRON

Cast iron can produce delightful results when baking and roasting. Check out my no-hassle tips for baking and roasting in a cast iron skillet or pan:

- **Preheat your cast iron:** Preheat your cast iron skillet or pan in the oven before baking or roasting. This will distribute the heat evenly.

- **Use parchment paper:** Line your cast iron skillet with parchment paper to keep food from sticking to the surface. This is especially useful for delicate baked goods such as cakes and cookies.

- **Watch your cooking time:** Cast iron retains heat well, so it may take less time to cook in it than other materials.

- **Grease the pan:** You may need to grease the pan before adding ingredients to prevent sticking. Use a small amount of butter or vegetable oil and spread it evenly over the pan's surface.

- **Avoid acidic ingredients:** Although cast iron is generally durable, it can react with acidic ingredients such as tomatoes and citrus fruits, causing a metallic taste.

By implementing these tips, you can enjoy the benefits of cast iron when baking or roasting, leading to delicious and uniformly cooked dishes.

SEASONING AND MAINTENANCE OF CAST IRON

BASICS OF THE SEASONING PROCESS

For your favorite frying pan to last you a long time, you need to season it. Despite its apparent ruggedness, the cast iron frying pan is quite delicate. But if you give it the proper care — which is quite simple — it will be a faithful helper for your family for generations to come. Here's why:

- **Non-stick surface:** The seasoning forms the natural non-stick surface of the cast iron skillet. A layer of polymerized oil creates a smooth coating that helps prevent food from sticking to the pan during cooking.

- **Improved heat distribution:** The seasoning also helps distribute heat over the entire surface of the pan, ensuring even cooking.

- **Rust-proof:** Cast iron is prone to rusting if not properly cared for. Seasoning creates a protective barrier on the surface of the pan, protecting it from moisture and preventing rust from forming.

- **Ease of care:** Seasoned cast iron pans are relatively easy to clean and maintain. The non-stick surface eliminates unnecessary cleaning, and the seasoning layer promotes easy removal of cooked food.

Easy steps you need to follow from time to time:

1. **Prepare the pan:** Wash the cast iron skillet with warm water and mild detergent, wiping it gently with a sponge or brush. Dry it thoroughly with a towel.

2. **Apply oil:** Apply a thin, even layer of food-safe oil or grease to the entire surface of the pan, including the handle. Vegetable oil, canola oil, or linseed oil are commonly used.

3. **Remove excess oil:** Use a paper towel or napkin to remove excess oil from the pan. The goal is to create a thin, almost invisible layer of oil.

4. **Preheat the pan:** Place it upside down in an oven preheated to 375⁰F (190⁰C). Be sure to place a baking sheet or aluminum foil on the bottom shelf to collect any oil drips.

5. **Baking process:** Leave the cast iron skillet to bake for about an hour. This will allow the oil to polymerize, creating a strong and non-stick coating on the surface.

6. **Cool and repeat:** After an hour, turn off the oven and allow the cast iron skillet to cool completely inside. Repeat the seasoning process a few more times, if desired, to further strengthen the seasoning layer.

Regular handling and proper care will keep your cast iron skillet seasoned and in great cooking condition for years to come.

CARE OF CAST IRON COOKWARE

Cleaning and caring for cast iron cookware is vital to preserve its properties and prevent rusting. Here's a step-by-step guide to cleaning and caring for your cast iron cookware:

Seasoning: Before using new cast iron cookware, or if your trusty old skillet needs to be retreated, apply a coat of oil to create a non-stick surface.

Daily cleaning:

- Allow cookware to cool completely after each use.
- Rinse with hot water, using a soft sponge or brush to remove food debris.
- Avoid using strong detergents, as they can remove the seasoning. However, if necessary, use a small amount of mild soap and rinse the cookware thoroughly.
- Dry the cast iron thoroughly with a towel or place them on the stove over low heat to allow any remaining moisture to evaporate.

Remove stubborn stains or residue:

- If stubborn stains or food residue stick to the cast iron, sprinkle coarse salt on the surface.
- Use a paper towel or soft brush to rub the salt onto the surface, pressing lightly.
- Rinse with hot water and dry thoroughly.

Avoiding rust:

- Avoiding rust is critical for cast iron. Always ensure the cookware is completely dry after cleaning to avoid moisture that can lead to rust.
- If you notice signs of rust, gently remove it with steel wool or a stiff brush. Once the rust is gone, follow the seasoning process described earlier to retreat the cookware.

Storage:

- Store cast iron cookware in a dry place with the lids off to allow proper air circulation.

- If you stack several items, you can place a paper or kitchen towel between them to prevent scratches.

Remember, the more often you use your cast iron cookware, the better it retains its magical properties. With proper care, cast iron cookware can last for generations, providing excellent cooking results for years to come.

COMMON MISTAKES IN CARING FOR CAST IRON

Although cast iron cookware is durable and long-lasting, people make several common mistakes when caring for it. Here are a few mistakes to avoid:

- **Using strong detergents or soaking in water for long periods:** Strong detergents and prolonged soaking can rob your cast iron cookware of its seasoning. Instead, use a small amount of mild soap and don't soak it for long periods. Clean it just after use to avoid the difficulty of removing food.

- **Cleaning with abrasive materials:** Avoid using harsh brushes, steel wool, or abrasive cleaners for cast iron cookware. They can damage the seasoning and surface. Instead, use a soft sponge, a nylon-bristle brush, or a gentle cleaner designed for cast iron.

- **Insufficient drying:** Proper drying of cast iron cookware is crucial to prevent rust. Leaving it to soak or not drying it thoroughly after washing it can lead to rust. Always make sure your cast iron is completely dry before putting it away.

- **Storing while still hot or wet:** Putting hot cast iron cookware directly into cold water or storing it while still warm can cause warping or cracking. Let the cookware cool completely before cleaning or storing it.

- **Storing without seasoning:** Cast iron cookware seasoning creates a protective layer and enhances its non-stick properties. Suppose you store cast iron cookware without seasoning or with a damaged layer of seasoning. In that case, it may rust and lose its non-stick properties over time. Season the cookware as needed, especially if you notice signs of rust or if the existing seasoning looks dull.

- **Cooking strongly acidic foods for long periods:** Cast iron is generally not recommended for cooking strongly acidic foods for long periods. Acidic ingredients can react with cast iron and affect the taste of the food. If you must cook acidic foods, try to keep cooking times to a minimum and ensure the cookware is well-soaked.

ADDITIONAL TOOLS FOR CAST IRON COOKING

Cast iron cooking gets a turbo-boost with these super helpful gadgets. Introducing a collection of handy-dandy tools that can enhance your cast iron cooking experience:

Cast iron scraper: The scraper is handy for cleaning up sticky food without damaging the seasoning. It has a flat, straight edge that easily removes stubborn food residue from the cooking surface.

Silicone handle pads: Cast iron handles can get extremely hot during cooking. Silicone handle pads provide heat protection and make it easier to handle your cookware safely. They fit over the handles and provide a comfortable grip.

Pot holders or oven mitts: When using cast iron cookware in the oven or on the stove, it's important to have pot holders or oven mitts to protect your hands from the heat. Look for durable options that can withstand high temperatures.

Grill pan press: If you like to grill in cast iron cookware, a grill pan press can be a valuable tool. This heavy, flat press helps grill meat and vegetables evenly while creating attractive grill marks.

A lid lifter for a cast iron Dutch oven: A lid lifter will come in handy if you have cookware with a heavy lid. The long handle lets you lift the hot lid easily and safely, even wearing gloves.

Chain scraper: This tool is effective for tough cleaning tasks or when removing stubborn residue. It is made of interlocking stainless-steel rings that gently scrape away stuck food without scratching the seasoning.

Long-handled tongs: These are useful when cooking with cast iron, especially when flipping dishes. Look for tongs with non-slip, heat-resistant handles.

Cast iron cookware trivets: These are sturdy tools designed to protect surfaces from heat damage caused by hot cast iron pans. They have a stable construction made of cast iron, stainless steel, or silicone. Trivets typically have an embossed, heat-resistant surface to distribute weight and heat evenly, preventing direct contact between the cookware and the surface. They come in various shapes and sizes; some can be adjusted or folded.

Select the tools that align with your unique cooking style and requirements to enhance the joy of your culinary explorations in cast iron.

Cozy Homemade Breakfasts

PANCAKES WITH HONEY AND BERRIES

Fresh pancakes for Sunday family breakfast are an American classic. They're quick and easy to cook, and there's no need to buy special ingredients. You probably already have everything you need in your pantry.

Pancakes made in cast iron with enough oil are the fluffiest and most buttery. Don't forget to add more oil between batches as the previous amount is absorbed.

You can experiment with the ingredients by substituting milk, yogurt, or even sour cream for the buttermilk — just be ready to adjust the amount of flour in this case. Wheat flour can also be replaced with grain or nut flour. Either way, cast iron will help you get the perfect, flavorful breakfast.

10 pancakes   7 minutes   20 minutes

INGREDIENTS:

- 2 cups (260 g) all-purpose flour
- 2¼ cups (540 ml) whole milk
- 1 medium egg
- 3 Tbsp. unsalted butter, melted
- ½ tsp. salt

- 1 Tbsp. sugar (optional)
- 1 Tbsp. baking powder
- ½ tsp. baking soda
- 2 Tbsp. olive oil, for the skillet

HOW TO COOK:

1. Preheat the cast-iron skillet over medium heat.
2. Mix all the ingredients using a mixer or blender. The better you whisk the batter, the fluffier your pancakes will be.
3. Heat olive oil in the skillet.
4. Pour ¼ cup (60 ml) of batter into the center of the skillet. Cook for 1-2 minutes on each side until golden brown.
5. Repeat with the remaining batter.
6. Serve pancakes hot with fresh berries and nuts, drizzling with liquid honey / maple syrup / Nutella / peanut butter, and topping with whipped cream.
7. Store pancakes in an airtight container in the fridge for up to 4 days. Reheat before serving.

NUTRITIONAL INFO (PER SERVING):

Calories: 194 Total Fat: 9.1 g, Chol: 31 mg, Sodium 117 mg, Total Carbs: 24.3 g, Dietary Fiber 0.7 g, Total Sugars 4.2 g, Protein: 5.0 g

Cozy Homemade Breakfasts

DUTCH BABY PANCAKE

Meet this puffy pancake that will become the go-to Sunday brunch for your family. It is very similar to the English pudding traditionally eaten with roast beef.

Suppose you omit the sugar and add some vegetables — you get a hearty breakfast. Grated cheese wouldn't be out of place, either. And instead of melted butter, fry some bacon and use the fat to grease the pan. You can choose to make it sweet or savory.

High-gluten flour works best for this recipe.

My children love this pancake with cranberry sauce, or applesauce washed down with milk.

3 servings   7 minutes   25 minutes

- ½ cup (60 g) all-purpose/bread flour
- ½ cup (120 ml) whole milk, at room temperature
- large eggs, at room temperature

- 4 Tbsp. unsalted butter, for the skillet
- 1 Tbsp. white sugar
- ½ tsp. vanilla extract / ¼ tsp. nutmeg / ¼ tsp. cinnamon

HOW TO COOK:

1. Ensure all the ingredients are at room temperature. It's crucial for this recipe.
2. Preheat the oven to 425⁰F (230⁰C).
3. Combine all the ingredients using a food processor/blender/mixer or by hand.
4. Preheat the skillet in the oven. Melt the butter in the hot skillet.
5. Pour the batter into the greased hot skillet.
6. Bake the pancake in the preheated oven for 15-20 minutes until golden.
7. Turn off the heat and let it sit there for 5 minutes. Remove from the oven and let it rest for another 2 minutes (it will come out of the skillet easier).
8. Serve hot, sprinkled with syrup or powdered sugar. It pairs perfectly with lemon, berries, sliced fruit, and a scoop of ice cream.

NUTRITIONAL INFO (PER SERVING):

Calories: 320 Total Fat: 21.3 g, Chol: 231 mg, Sodium 195 mg, Total Carbs: 21.2 g, Dietary Fiber 0.7 g, Total Sugars 7.3 g, Protein: 9.7 g

SPINACH FRITTATA WITH PINE NUTS

Wow, one more dish with countless variations of toppings. You can add shredded boiled chicken, broccoli florets, chopped bell pepper, sliced zucchini, halved cherry tomatoes, sliced yellow onion, peas, or corn. It's hard for me to imagine a combination you wouldn't like. The basic rule is that the toppings should be semi-cooked before adding the egg mixture.

The cast-iron pan gives the frittata a sponge-like texture. And it's very handy to pre-cook the toppings in one pan and put the same pan into the oven for the final cooking.

4　　　　　　10 minutes　　　25 minutes

INGREDIENTS:

- 4 medium eggs
- 3 Tbsp. heavy cream
- ⅓ cup (40 g) feta cheese, crumbled
- 4 cremini mushrooms, sliced
- 4 Tbsp. baby spinach
- 2 scallions, roughly chopped

- ⅓ cup (20 g) parmesan, grated
- ½ tsp. garlic powder
- salt and pepper, to taste
- 1 Tbsp. roasted pine nuts, for sprinkling
- 1 Tbsp. olive oil

HOW TO COOK:

1. Preheat your oven to 400⁰F (205⁰C).
2. Whisk heavy cream with eggs, garlic powder, salt, and pepper.
3. Heat olive oil in the cast-iron skillet over medium-low. Add the chopped scallions, sliced mushrooms, and spinach. Cook for 5 minutes until tender. Remove from heat.
4. Add crumbled feta cheese.
5. Pour the egg mixture into the skillet and sprinkle with grated Parmesan.
6. Cook in the preheated oven for 15-20 minutes.
7. Sprinkle with pine nuts and serve as a main or side dish with a juicy steak.

NUTRITIONAL INFO (PER SERVING):

Calories: 198, Total Carbs: 3.2 g, Total Fat: 16.4 g, Chol: 192 mg, Sodium 228 mg, Protein: 9.5 g, Fiber: 0.5 g, Sugar: 1.5 g

SWEET POTATO HASH WITH EGGS

This tender hash is as healthy as it is delicious. The caramelized sweetness of fried sweet potatoes pairs well with tender eggs. Eggs and chunks of bacon make the vegetable bed rich in protein.

Sometimes I substitute Italian sausages for the bacon — my kids like it better that way. If you don't have much time, you can use pre-cooked sweet potatoes (or any other kind of potato), but they are certainly tastier when steeped in the bacon flavor.

You can add chopped spinach or kale at the end of the frying if desired.

2   10 minutes   35 minutes

- 4 slices bacon (60 g), chopped
- 1 large (100 g) sweet potato, peeled and chopped
- 1 bell pepper (140 g), chopped
- 1 small onion (50 g), coarsely chopped
- 3 Tbsp. olive oil
- Salt and pepper, to taste
- 1 Tbsp. salted butter
- 4 large eggs
- 1 tsp. garlic powder

HOW TO COOK:

1. Heat a cast-iron pan over medium heat.
2. Add chopped bacon and cook until crispy. Remove bacon from the pan.
3. Add chopped onion and bell peppers to the pan and cook for 2-3 minutes until tender. If there isn't enough fat from the bacon to fry the vegetables, then add some butter or oil.
4. Add chopped sweet potato, garlic powder, salt, and pepper. Cook for 15 minutes, stirring often. Cover the pan with a lid and sauté for 5 minutes.
5. Return the bacon to the pan and stir.
6. Make four hollows in the hash and break an egg into each one. Cook until the eggs are set. You can use a lid to speed up the process.
7. Serve sprinkled with freshly crushed pepper and chopped greens.

NUTRITIONAL INFO (PER SERVING):

Calories: 597, Total Fat: 46 g, Saturated Fat: 13.7 g, Chol: 417 mg, Sodium 642 mg, Total Carbs: 19.9 g, Dietary Fiber 3.4 g, Total Sugars: 8.5 g, Protein: 24.9 g, Calcium 71 mg, Iron 4 mg, Potassium 552 mg

Cozy Homemade Breakfasts

STUFFED FRENCH TOASTS

If you love to eat French toast and even prepare it outdoors with your favorite cast iron, try making stuffed French toast. This simple upgrade will make your breakfast extra special.

You can use any berry jam or marmalade for the stuffing but choose a bright flavor. The mascarpone will soften it a bit, and along with the fluffy, eggy bread, it will taste like a complete dessert.

6   10 minutes   7 minutes

INGREDIENTS:

- 6 thick slices (1-inch / 2.5 cm) white bread / brioche / challah
- 4 medium eggs
- 1 cup (240 ml) whole milk
- 2 Tbsp. white sugar
- A pinch of salt
- ¼ tsp. ground cinnamon
- ⅛ tsp. nutmeg
- ½ tsp. vanilla extract

- 4 Tbsp. butter / ghee
- 2 lemon wedges
- 12 sliced strawberries, for serving

FOR THE STUFFING:

- ¾ cup (180 g) mascarpone
- 1½ Tbsp. powdered sugar
- 2 Tbsp. heavy cream
- 1 cup (240 ml) strawberry / orange jelly / marmalade

HOW TO COOK:

1. Cut a pocket in each bread slice. Be sure to use bread that is 1 to 2 days old.

2. Whisk together eggs, milk, sugar, salt, and spices.

3. Preheat a cast-iron griddle or large skillet over medium heat.

4. Blend together mascarpone, powdered sugar, and heavy cream. Carefully stuff the bread pockets with the mascarpone mixture and berry jam.

5. Grease the skillet with butter. Coat the stuffed bread slices with the egg-milk mixture and arrange them in the preheated skillet. Toast them on each side until golden brown.

6. Transfer the toasts to the serving platter and let rest for 2-3 minutes. Serve sprinkled with lemon juice and topped with fresh strawberry slices.

NUTRITIONAL INFO (PER SERVING):

Calories 459, Total Fat 24.6 g, Saturated Fat 14.2 g, Chol: 202 mg, Sodium 292 mg, Total Carbs: 51.6 g, Dietary Fiber 1.4 g, Total Sugars 37.5 g, Protein 11.2 g, Calcium 157 mg, Iron 1 mg, Potassium 191 mg

Cozy Homemade Breakfasts

Seafood Dedights

SEAFOOD PAELLA

Paella is an Arabic-Spanish dish with a rice base that is perfect for add-ins selected from leftovers from your fridge. You can use any grain you choose, but rice is perfect because it has a neutral taste and absorbs spicy, rich flavors from the add-ins.

I share the easiest way to cook paella at home using your cast-iron pan, but you can upgrade the recipe by adding chorizo, various seafood, fish chunks (cod, halibut), or even meat. Of course, the recipe requires frying these elements before adding them to the rice, but I simplified the recipe. Gourmets can follow the traditional method and get excellent results.

6   15 minutes   50 minutes

INGREDIENTS:

- 1½ cups (300 g) short-grain rice (Bomba, Calasparra, Arborio)
- 3 cups (720 ml) chicken stock, hot
- 1 pinch of saffron thread
- 1 lb. (450 g) shrimp/prawns, peeled and deveined
- ½ lb. (225 g) mussels, scrubbed and debearded
- 1 red onion (70 g), chopped

- 3 garlic cloves, minced
- 2 tomatoes, chopped
- ½ cup (80 g) frozen peas, thawed
- 3 Tbsp. olive oil
- 1 tsp. smoked paprika
- ½ tsp. red pepper flakes
- 6 oz. (170 g) green beans
- ⅓ cup fresh parsley, chopped
- Sea salt, to taste

HOW TO COOK:

1. Heat olive oil in a large, deep, cast-iron pan over medium heat.

2. Add chopped onion and cook for 2 minutes until tender. Add rice and cook for 3 minutes, stirring often.

3. Add minced garlic, chopped tomatoes, green beans, peas, saffron thread, paprika, and red pepper flakes and cook for 1 minute, stirring often.

4. Add 2 cups of chicken stock and bring to a boil. Cook for 5-10 minutes, stirring occasionally.

5. Reduce the heat to low, cover with a lid, and simmer for 20 minutes.

6. Open the lid, stir in shrimp and mussels, close the lid, and cook for 10 minutes. Add stock or water if needed.

7. Serve warm with lemon wedges.

NUTRITIONAL INFO (PER SERVING):

Calories 844, Total Fat 10.6 g, Saturated Fat 2 g, Chol: 168 mg, Sodium 697 mg, Total Carbs: 146 g, Dietary Fiber 5.4 g, Total Sugars 3.5 g, Protein 36 g, Calcium 163 mg, Iron 10 mg, Potassium 683 mg

Seafood Delights

PAN SEARED SCALLOPS

Fans of restaurant-quality seafood will love this exceptionally easy scallop recipe. Be sure to use dry scallops to get a golden crust.

Seared, crusted scallops pair with fried Brussels sprouts, creamy pasta, mashed cauliflower, vegetable risotto, roasted vegetables, etc.

| 2 | 5 minutes | 5 minutes |

INGREDIENTS:

- ½ lb. (225 g) dry sea scallops
- 3 Tbsp. unsalted butter/ghee
- Sea salt and pepper, to taste

HOW TO COOK:

1. Preheat a cast-iron skillet over medium heat.
2. Meanwhile, pat the scallops dry. Season them with salt and pepper.
3. Melt the butter in the skillet and arrange the scallops in the pan in a single layer.
4. Cook for 2 minutes on each side.
5. Transfer to a serving platter and serve with lemon wedges.

NUTRITIONAL INFO (PER SERVING):

Calories 252, Total Fat 18.1 g, Saturated Fat 11 g, Chol: 83 mg, Sodium 304 mg, Total Carbs: 2.7 g, Dietary Fiber 0 g, Total Sugars 0 g, Protein 19.2 g, Calcium 32 mg, Iron 0 mg, Potassium 367 mg

Seafood Delights

SEARED SALMON WITH VEGETABLES

This one-pan salmon recipe is dinner-worthy for the whole family. You can upgrade it by replacing the vegetable stock with creamy garlic sauce or substituting asparagus, spinach, or green beans for the broccoli.

The whole point of cooking in one pan is to mix the juices and flavors of the salmon with the vegetables. Serve sprinkled with fresh parsley or chopped scallions.

6   15 minutes   25 minutes

INGREDIENTS:

- 1½ lb. (680 g) salmon fillet, cut into strips
- 1 Tbsp. canola oil, divided
- Salt and pepper, to taste
- 1 cup (70 g) broccoli florets
- 1 cup (70 g) cauliflower florets
- ½ lb. (225 g) baby potatoes, halved
- 1½ cups (360 ml) vegetable stock, hot
- 2 Tbsp. lemon juice

HOW TO COOK:

1. Preheat the oven to 350⁰F (175⁰C).

2. Meanwhile, heat canola oil in a large cast-iron pan over medium heat.

3. Season salmon strips with salt and pepper and fry for 2-3 minutes on each side. Remove from pan and set aside.

4. Add vegetables to the pan and season with salt and pepper. Cook for 5 minutes, stirring occasionally.

5. Return fried salmon to the pan and add hot vegetable stock and lemon juice. Bake uncovered in the oven for 15 minutes.

6. Let it rest, covered, for 10 minutes before serving.

NUTRITIONAL INFO (PER SERVING):

Calories 205, Total Fat 10 g, Saturated Fat 1.7 g, Chol: 50 mg, Sodium 245 mg, Total Carbs: 7.2 g, Dietary Fiber 1.8 g, Total Sugars 1.3 g, Protein 23.7 g, Calcium 62 mg, Iron 2 mg, Potassium 695 mg

Seafood Delights

CAJUN SHRIMP ETOUFFEE

This New Orleans classic is none other than vegetables in shrimp sauce. I'm sharing my Cajun seasoning recipe, but you can use a store-bought one as a quick alternative. The list of ingredients is impressive, but it's all very easy and quick to make and very helpful at my fall family dinners.

The biggest challenge is making the right roux. It should resemble peanut butter in color and have a nutty smell. If you burn it, you will have to throw it away and start over. Have some patience, or just buy a ready-made one.

6   15 minutes   25 minutes

INGREDIENTS:

- ½ cup (65 g) all-purpose flour
- ½ cup (120 ml) sesame / canola oil
- 1 yellow onion (70 g), chopped
- 1 bell pepper (140 g), chopped
- ¾ cup celery stalks, chopped
- 2 jalapenos, chopped
- 1 tomato, chopped
- 10 garlic cloves, minced
- 1½ seafood stock, hot
- 2 bay leaves
- 2 Tbsp. hot sauce
- 2 lb. (900 g) shrimp, peeled and deveined

- 2 Tbsp. salted butter
- ½ cup scallions, chopped
- 2 cups (300 g) rice, cooked

FOR THE CAJUN SEASONING:

- ½ tsp. dried thyme
- ½ tsp. dried oregano
- ½ tsp. garlic powder
- ½ tsp. onion powder
- ¼ tsp. cayenne pepper
- ¼ tsp. black pepper
- ¼ tsp. white pepper
- 1 tsp. smoked paprika

HOW TO COOK:

1. Heat sesame oil and butter in a large cast-iron pot over medium heat.
2. Add flour and cook for 8-10 minutes until light brown, stirring constantly. Take care not to burn it.
3. Once you smell the nutty aroma, add the onions, tomato, bell peppers, jalapenos, garlic, and celery, and simmer for 5 minutes, stirring occasionally.
4. Add seafood stock, 2 tablespoons of Cajun seasoning, hot sauce, and bay leaves, and bring to a boil. Cook for 15 minutes over low heat. Add shrimp and cook for 5 minutes.
5. Remove the étouffée from the heat, take out the bay leaves, and let it cool for 10 minutes. Serve sprinkled with chopped scallions on a bed of rice.

NUTRITIONAL INFO (PER SERVING):

Calories 540, Total Fat 25.6 g, Saturated Fat 6 g, Chol: 327 mg, Sodium 626 mg, Total Carbs: 36.1 g, Dietary Fiber 2.4 g, Total Sugars 2.5 g, Protein 39.2 g, Calcium 177 mg, Iron 7 mg, Potassium 570 mg

Seafood Delights

TILAPIA WITH TOMATO SAUCE

This recipe takes inspiration from Mediterranean cuisine. Turn to this thick, tomato-based sauce with firm white fish to shake up your weekend dinners. Choose seasonal vegetables grown by local farmers so they reveal their best flavors in the dish. Fleshy, juicy tomatoes (such as Beefsteak, Brandywine, Saucy Lady, etc.) work best in this recipe.

Serve on a bed of your favorite grain or with crusty bread you can dip in the sauce.

6   10 minutes   40 minutes

INGREDIENTS:

- 2 lb. (900 g) tilapia / cod / halibut fillets
- 2 Tbsp. olive oil
- 1 red onion (70 g), diced
- 1 bell pepper (140 g), diced
- 2 garlic cloves, minced
- ½ cup (90 g) green olives, diced

- 3 large ripe tomatoes (700 g), peeled and chopped
- 3 tsp. dried thyme
- 1 tsp. smoked paprika
- ⅓ cup (80 ml) lemon juice
- Salt and pepper, to taste

HOW TO COOK:

1. Preheat the oven to 400⁰F (205⁰C).

2. Meanwhile, heat olive oil in a large cast-iron pan over medium heat. Add diced onion and cook for 5 minutes until tender, stirring occasionally.

3. Add tomatoes, garlic, diced bell pepper, salt, and pepper. Adjust heat to maintain a simmer. Cook for 15 minutes, stirring occasionally.

4. Mix lemon juice, dried thyme, paprika, salt, and pepper. Brush the tilapia fillets with the marinade. Let it stand for 10 minutes.

5. Immerse the fish in the sauce, add diced olives, and bake for 20 minutes.

6. Serve warm over pasta or rice.

NUTRITIONAL INFO (PER SERVING):

Calories 209, Total Fat 7.6 g, Saturated Fat 1.7 g, Chol: 73 mg, Sodium 152 mg, Total Carbs: 8.5 g, Dietary Fiber 2.4 g, Total Sugars 4.5 g, Protein 29.6 g, Calcium 64 mg, Iron 3 mg, Potassium 314 mg

Seafood Delights

Comforting Poultry Courses

ROASTED CHICKEN WITH POTATOES

This is an easy, very moist, and absolutely delicious way to prepare chicken with crispy potatoes. The potatoes soak up the juices and fat of the chicken, the flavor of the garlic, and the aroma of spicy herbs. You can upgrade the dish by adding carrots, onions, lemon zest, and lemon juice.

If the potatoes are not quite cooked, but the chicken is done, take the chicken out and let it rest on a cutting board while you return the skillet with the potatoes to the oven.

Leftovers make great chicken sandwiches.

6   15 minutes   60 minutes

- 3-4 lb. (1.5-1.8 Kg) whole chicken
- 1½ lb. (675 g) potatoes, peeled and cut into wedges
- 3 garlic cloves, diced

- 2 Tbsp. salted butter, melted
- 2 Tbsp. olive oil
- 1 Tbsp. dried thyme
- 1 Tbsp. dried rosemary
- Salt and pepper, to taste

1. Preheat the oven to 425°F (220°C). Heat a 12-inch (30 cm) cast-iron skillet in the oven.

2. Pat the chicken dry and rub it with thyme, salt, and pepper.

3. Mix potatoes with diced garlic, melted butter, salt, pepper, rosemary, thyme, and 1 tablespoon of olive oil.

4. Place the chicken in the skillet and arrange the potatoes around it.

5. Roast for 50-60 minutes until chicken and potatoes are golden brown.

6. Let it stand for 15 minutes before transferring to a cutting board.

7. Serve the carved chicken with potatoes and a fresh salad.

Calories 588, Total Fat 25.6 g, Saturated Fat 7.7 g, Chol: 212 mg, Sodium 231 mg, Total Carbs: 18.8 g, Dietary Fiber 3.1 g, Total Sugars 1.5 g, Protein 67.2 g, Calcium 64 mg, Iron 4 mg, Potassium 1025 mg

CHICKEN POTPIE

Classic chicken potpie is a top-rated meal in North America. Because of its simplicity and popularity, it has a lot of variations. Some like it spicy, and they add Cajun spices or herbs, some like it nutritious, and they use the additional bottom crust. Any leftovers in your fridge can be used as a filling — mushrooms, beans, onions, bacon, etc.

Everybody seems to like the creamy sauce for the filling. You can adjust the amount of milk/broth to achieve your preferred texture.

| 6 | 15 minutes | 40 minutes |

INGREDIENTS:

- 2 pre-cooked chicken breasts (350 g), shredded
- 3 Tbsp. salted butter
- 3 Tbsp. all-purpose flour
- 2 cups (480 ml) whole milk / chicken broth
- ½ cup (80 g) peas

- ½ cup (80 g) frozen corn
- 1 small carrot (70 g), diced
- 1 potato (60 g), peeled and chopped
- 1 cup (240 ml) cream
- 1 pre-made piecrust
- Salt and pepper, to taste

HOW TO COOK:

1. Preheat the oven to 400⁰F (205⁰C).

2. Melt salted butter in a 12-inch (30 cm) cast-iron skillet over medium heat.

3. Add the flour and stir for 2 minutes. Add shredded chicken, potato, peas, diced carrots, milk, and cream. Cook for 5 minutes, stirring occasionally.

4. Remove the skillet from the heat and cover with the piecrust, making 4 vapor vents.

5. Bake for 30 minutes until golden brown.

6. Let the pie stand for 15 minutes before serving.

NUTRITIONAL INFO (PER SERVING):

Calories 288, Total Fat 16 g, Saturated Fat 7.7 g, Chol: 73 mg, Sodium 153 mg, Total Carbs: 19.1 g, Dietary Fiber 2 g, Total Sugars 6.5 g, Protein 19.2 g, Calcium 120 mg, Iron 2 mg, Potassium 468 mg

Comforting Poultry Courses

CHICKEN AND SAUSAGE JAMBALAYA

A flavorful Louisiana-style dish in which chicken, sausage, vegetables, and rice are cooked together in a cast-iron skillet until the rice is tender and full of spice. I make it so often that I can do it blindfolded. For my family, I make it less spicy and add a medley of seafood — but some of us like it hot!

You can upgrade the recipe by adjusting the ingredients — add more tomatoes, use less chicken, add shrimp, use more garlic, add dried basil... you name it. Fresh-baked cornbread muffins or garlic bread are perfect additions to jambalaya.

6   15 minutes   60 minutes

INGREDIENTS:

- 2 Tbsp. olive oil / avocado oil, divided
- 1 Tbsp. Cajun seasoning, divided
- 10 oz. (280 g) chorizo, sliced
- 1 lb. (450 g) chicken fillets, cut into chunks
- 1 yellow onion (70 g), chopped
- 1 bell pepper, chopped
- 2 celery stalks, diced

- 3 garlic cloves, crushed
- 1 can (16 oz. (450 g) or bigger) plum tomatoes
- ⅓ tsp. red pepper flakes
- ½ tsp. hot pepper sauce
- Salt and pepper, to taste
- 1¼ cup (230 g) uncooked long-grain rice (jasmine/basmati)
- 2½ cups (600 ml) chicken broth

HOW TO COOK:

1. Heat 1 tablespoon olive oil in a large cast-iron pan / Dutch oven over medium heat.

2. Fry chicken chunks with half of the Cajun seasoning until browned. Remove from the pan and set aside.

3. Add sliced chorizo, chopped onion, bell pepper, celery, and garlic to the pan. Cook for 5 minutes until tender.

4. Add crushed tomatoes, fried chicken, red pepper flakes, salt, and pepper. Simmer for 10 minutes, stirring occasionally.

5. Add rice and chicken broth and bring to a boil. Cover tightly with the lid. Reduce heat to low and cook for 25-35 minutes, stirring occasionally. Check the rice for readiness.

NUTRITIONAL INFO (PER SERVING):

Calories 754, Total Fat 29.6 g, Saturated Fat 9.3 g, Chol: 102 mg, Sodium 1010 mg, Total Carbs: 75.9 g, Dietary Fiber 2.4 g, Total Sugars 4.5 g, Protein 42.2 g, Calcium 61 mg, Iron 6 mg, Potassium 821 mg

Comforting Poultry Courses

CAST IRON CHICKEN PARMESAN

I originally made these creamy chicken breasts with mushrooms and artichoke hearts, but I like sun-dried tomatoes so much that I add them to almost all my dishes. That's how this recipe was born. Also, inspired by Mediterranean cuisine, I use white wine instead of chicken broth. You can try making it this way, too. It's not really even a recipe but a culinary idea combining chicken, heavy cream, and cheese into a winning combination.

Be sure to pat the chicken breasts dry before frying for a crispy golden crust.

4   15 minutes   40 minutes

- 4 chicken breast halves, skinless
- 1 Tbsp. olive oil
- 2 garlic cloves, minced
- 1 Tbsp. dried oregano
- ½ tbsp. paprika
- ¾ cup (180 ml) chicken broth

- ½ cup (120 ml) heavy cream
- ½ cup sun-dried tomatoes, chopped
- 1 cup fresh spinach leaves/kale
- ¼ cup (15 g) parmesan/Gruyere, shredded
- Salt and pepper, to taste

HOW TO COOK:

1. Preheat the oven to 350°F (175°C).
2. Heat olive oil in a cast-iron skillet over medium heat.
3. Season chicken breasts with salt and pepper. Cook in the skillet until golden on each side. Set them aside.
4. Add minced garlic, oregano, and paprika to the skillet and cook for 1 minute, stirring often.
5. Add chicken broth, heavy cream, chopped sun-dried tomatoes, spinach, and shredded Parmesan. Season with salt and pepper. Bring to a simmer.
6. Immerse the chicken breasts in the sauce and put the skillet into the oven.
7. Bake for 15-20 minutes.
8. Creamy Parmesan chicken is an ideal pairing with whatever delicious side dish or pasta you like to serve.

NUTRITIONAL INFO (PER SERVING):

Calories 374, Total Fat 24.3 g, Saturated Fat 10.7 g, Chol: 129 mg, Sodium 1249 mg, Total Carbs: 7.1 g, Dietary Fiber 1.4 g, Total Sugars 2.5 g, Protein 33.2 g, Calcium 116 mg, Iron 2 mg, Potassium 202 mg

DUCK BREAST WITH RASPBERRY SAUCE

Fried duck breast with berry sauce is the most effortless way to create a gourmet dish for a special dinner. Just a few ingredients, and you get a taste feast in a few minutes. The caramelized sweetness of the fried duck plays well with the sour-sweet raspberry sauce. Serve with duck-fat roasted potatoes or braised cabbage.

You can decrease the sweetness of the breast by adjusting the amount of sugar and cinnamon.

4   10 minutes   20 minutes

- 4 duck breast halves, boneless
- Salt and pepper, to taste
- 4 oz. (115 g) raspberries
- 1 tsp. ground cinnamon
- 1 Tbsp. dark brown sugar

- ½ cup (120 ml) dry red / raspberry wine
- 1 tsp. cornstarch
- 1 tsp. salt
- ¼ cup (60 ml) raspberry liqueur

============================ HOW TO COOK: ============================

1. Using a sharp knife, make diagonal, diamond-shaped incisions across the fatty part of the duck breast. Make deep incisions, but do not cut through the flesh, only the fat. Season the breasts with salt and pepper.

2. Preheat a large cast-iron pan over medium heat. Sear the breasts for 4-5 minutes on each side until golden brown.

3. Meanwhile, combine brown sugar, cinnamon, and salt in a small bowl.

4. Transfer the fried breasts to a serving platter and sprinkle with the sugar mixture.

5. Combine red wine, liqueur, and cornstarch in a small saucepan and simmer for 2-3 minutes. Add raspberries and cook for another 2-3 minutes until thickened.

6. Caramelize the duck breasts skin side up on the skillet for 1 minute.

7. Slice thinly and drizzle with raspberry sauce.

============================ NUTRITIONAL INFO (PER SERVING): ============================

Calories 407, Total Fat 9.8 g, Saturated Fat 0 g, Chol: 0 mg, Sodium 1171 mg, Total Carbs: 7.5 g, Dietary Fiber 2.4 g, Total Sugars 15.7 g, Protein 53.2 g, Calcium 17 mg, Iron 0 mg, Potassium 78 mg

Delectable Main Courses

Baked Mac & Cheese	62
Braised Brussels Sprouts with Bacon	64
Sausage With Vegetables	66
Spinach Artichoke Dip	68
Buffalo Chicken Dip	70

BAKED MAC & CHEESE

Mac and cheese is the king of side dishes in our family. This real comfort dish is so good that I build my entire dinner around it. I pick which meats or vegetables go well with it, but it still outshines them all. It is loved even by those who don't care for pasta.

This dish is very simple to make — start with a béchamel sauce, add spices and cheese, stir in the macaroni, and bake in the oven until golden. If you like a crispy crust, sprinkle it with breadcrumbs and butter mixture before baking.

| 4 | 10 minutes | 35 minutes |

- 8 oz. (225 g) cooked macaroni (penne, elbows, fusilli, ziti), al dente
- 3 Tbsp. unsalted butter
- 2 Tbsp. all-purpose flour
- 2 cups (480 ml) warm whole milk
- ½ tsp. onion powder

- ½ tsp. garlic powder
- ½ tsp. red pepper flakes
- 1 cup (60 g) cheddar / Gruyere, shredded
- 1 cup (60 g) jack cheese / parmesan/smoked Gouda, shredded
- Salt and pepper, to taste

HOW TO COOK:

1. Preheat the oven to 375⁰F (190⁰C).
2. Melt butter in a large cast-iron skillet over low heat. Stir in flour and cook for 1 minute, stirring constantly.
3. Add the milk a little at a time, stirring constantly. Simmer for 4 minutes until thickened. Stir in seasonings, salt, and pepper, and cook for 2 minutes.
4. Add cheeses and cook until melted and combined, stirring constantly.
5. Add pasta and stir to combine. Bake for 20-25 minutes until golden.
6. Sprinkle with fresh parsley and serve with grilled meat or vegetables.

NUTRITIONAL INFO (PER SERVING):

Calories 475, Total Fat 17.6 g, Saturated Fat 10.7 g, Chol: 47 mg, Sodium 460 mg, Total Carbs: 52.5 g, Dietary Fiber 2 g, Total Sugars 8.5 g, Protein 25.7 g, Calcium 389 mg, Iron 2 mg, Potassium 356 mg

BRAISED BRUSSELS SPROUTS WITH BACON

I can't say that this dish combines completely incongruous ingredients, but even those who don't like Brussels sprouts are happy to eat them with fried bacon. They say the cabbage flavor completely disappears. It's hard to argue with that because I love crispy Brussels sprouts as much as I love bacon, but there's definitely some magic in this simple dish.

Braised Brussels sprouts can be a great side dish as well as a main dish. You can customize this dish by adding caramelized onions, cashews, Portobello mushrooms, bell peppers, or even maple syrup.

2   10 minutes   15 minutes

INGREDIENTS:

- 1 lb. (450 g) Brussels sprouts, halved
- 4 slices thick bacon (80 g), diced
- 2 garlic cloves, diced
- ½ cup (120 ml) chicken / turkey stock

- 1 Tbsp. salted butter
- 1 Tbsp. lemon juice / balsamic vinegar
- Salt and pepper, to taste
- Fresh rosemary, for garnish

HOW TO COOK:

1. Fry bacon chunks in a 12-inch (30 cm) cast-iron pan over medium heat for 5 minutes until starting to crisp. Set bacon chunks aside.

2. Set the heat to high. Add halved Brussels sprouts to the pan with bacon grease and cook for 3 minutes until lightly brown, stirring occasionally.

3. Add diced garlic and cook for 1 minute, stirring occasionally.

4. Pour in chicken stock and simmer, covered, for 4 minutes. Remove the lid and continue to cook for 4 minutes until the sprouts are tender, stirring occasionally.

5. Remove from the heat and add bacon, lemon juice, and salted butter. Season with salt and pepper and mix.

6. Garnish with fresh rosemary and serve with mashed potatoes or grilled pork chops.

NUTRITIONAL INFO (PER SERVING):

Calories 297, Total Fat 16.6 g, Saturated Fat 8 g, Chol: 45 mg, Sodium 731 mg, Total Carbs: 21.8 g, Dietary Fiber 8.4 g, Total Sugars 5.2 g, Protein 18.2 g, Calcium 83 mg, Iron 3 mg, Potassium 901 mg

SAUSAGE WITH VEGETABLES

On the list of comfort foods, fried sausages are somewhere near the top. They don't just add protein to the vegetables, they saturate the entire dish with savory juices, making it whole. This sausage skillet is a perfect solution for meal prep — quick to make and easy to reheat.

If your sausages are too spicy, adjust the amount of salt and seasonings in the recipe. For a stew-like consistency, add some chicken broth to the vegetables.

4   10 minutes   15 minutes

- 12 oz. (340 g) pre-cooked sausage (Italian / Cajun / Andouille), diced
- 1 bell pepper (150 g), diced
- 1 yellow onion (80 g), diced
- 1 zucchini, diced
- 2 cups (330 g) corn kernels (optional)
- 1 Tbsp. olive oil
- ½ tsp. smoked paprika
- ¼ cup green onion, chopped

HOW TO COOK:

1. Heat olive oil in a cast-iron skillet over medium heat.
2. Add diced sausages and cook for 4 minutes on each side until golden brown.
3. Remove the sausages and set aside.
4. Add diced vegetables to the skillet and cook for 5 minutes, stirring occasionally.
5. Return sausages to the skillet and stir in. Add smoked paprika and cook for 2 minutes, stirring once.
6. Sprinkle with chopped green onion and serve with quinoa or crispy garlic bread.

NUTRITIONAL INFO (PER SERVING):

Calories 467, Total Fat 30.1 g, Saturated Fat 8.7 g, Chol: 74 mg, Sodium 684 mg, Total Carbs: 31 g, Dietary Fiber 5.4 g, Total Sugars 7.5 g, Protein 22.2 g, Calcium 33 mg, Iron 5 mg, Potassium 849 mg

SPINACH ARTICHOKE DIP

I don't provide appetizer recipes in this book. This is understandable because cast-iron cookware is about substantial cooking, large quantities, and hearty dishes. But this dip is very different from all the light, pre-dinner appetizers out there. Its high cheese content with artichoke pieces makes it a complete meal.

Of course, it can be served at parties and family gatherings.

6   10 minutes   50 minutes

INGREDIENTS:

- 16 oz. (450 g) cream cheese, softened
- 1½ lb. (680 g) fresh spinach, chopped
- 10 oz. (280 g) marinated artichoke hearts, chopped
- 1 white onion (70 g), chopped
- 1 cup (240 ml) sour cream / Greek yogurt

- 1 cup (60 g) parmesan, grated
- 8 oz. (226 g) mozzarella, crumbled
- 4 garlic cloves, minced
- ¼ tsp. nutmeg
- ½ tsp. salt
- ½ tsp. white pepper
- 2 Tbsp. olive oil

HOW TO COOK:

1. Preheat the oven to 350°F (175°C). Grease a 12-inch (30 cm) cast-iron skillet with olive oil.
2. Mix all ingredients thoroughly in a large bowl.
3. Spread the artichoke mixture in the skillet and bake for 50 minutes until golden brown.
4. Serve warm with vegetable wedges or pita chips for dipping or as a topping for bruschetta toast.

NUTRITIONAL INFO (PER SERVING):

Calories 534, Total Fat 40.6 g, Saturated Fat 20.1 g, Chol: 82 mg, Sodium 971 mg, Total Carbs: 17.6 g, Dietary Fiber 3 g, Total Sugars 15.5 g, Protein 27 g, Calcium 550 mg, Iron 3 mg, Potassium 725 mg

BUFFALO CHICKEN DIP

As a chef should, I know cheese and love to savor it in its purest form — but I like cooking with cheese even more. Only a few varieties of this popular dairy product are suitable for baking. Cheddar, Parmesan, and Gruyere are the undisputed leaders in creating a tender, creamy texture, and they go well with almost all types of meat, vegetables, and bread.

The chicken can be replaced with shredded vegetables, bread, or nothing at all, and you'll still have a great, flavorful dish.

4   10 minutes   25 minutes

INGREDIENTS:

- 2 cups (300 g) pre-cooked chicken/ rotisserie chicken, shredded
- ½ cup (120 ml) hot pepper sauce / Buffalo sauce
- 1 Tbsp. unsalted butter
- 1 tsp. lemon juice
- 4 Tbsp. sour cream / Greek yogurt / ranch dressing

- 4 oz. (115 g) cream cheese, softened
- ½ cup (30 g) Cheddar cheese, freshly grated
- ¼ cup (20 g) blue cheese, crumbled
- 1 Tbsp. green onion, chopped

HOW TO COOK:

1. Preheat the oven to 375⁰F (190⁰C).
2. Melt the butter in an 8-inch (20 cm) cast-iron skillet over medium heat.
3. Add shredded chicken and hot sauce and cook for 3 minutes, stirring occasionally.
4. Remove the skillet from the heat. Stir in lemon juice, sour cream, cream cheese, and grated Cheddar.
5. Bake for 10-13 minutes until bubbling and golden brown.
6. Sprinkle with crumbled blue cheese and chopped green onion.
7. Serve with vegetable wedges, crispy bread, or crackers.

NUTRITIONAL INFO (PER SERVING):

Calories 354, Total Fat 24.6 g, Saturated Fat 14.7 g, Chol: 119 mg, Sodium 1321 mg, Total Carbs: 3.8 g, Dietary Fiber 1.1 g, Total Sugars 0.5 g, Protein 28.2 g, Calcium 194 mg, Iron 1 mg, Potassium 224 mg

Meat Extravaganza

Meat Extravaganza

SKILLET LASAGNA

The cast iron lasagna recipe is easier than the original version but is just as delicious. This winter dish is popular in our family — even in hot July. Moreover, in the summer, I add seasonal vegetables to it, which we gladly buy at our local farmers' market. Spinach, carrots, and bell peppers work perfectly here.

Thanks to its quick preparation, lasagna has seamlessly migrated from special occasions to any day of the week. And a large skillet helps provide school lunches for the kids for several days.

4   15 minutes   50 minutes

INGREDIENTS:

- 1 lb. (450 g) ground beef
- 2 cups (450 g) mozzarella, grated
- 1 cup (250 g) cottage cheese / ricotta
- 2 Tbsp. olive oil
- 1 white onion (70 g), chopped
- 3 garlic cloves, minced

- 1½ lb. (680 g) marinara sauce / basil pasta sauce
- 1 Tbsp. herbs de Provence
- 8 lasagna noodles, broken into 4 pieces each
- 1 cup fresh parsley, chopped

HOW TO COOK:

1. Preheat the oven to 400°F (205°C).
2. Heat olive oil in a 12-inch (30 cm) cast-iron skillet over medium-low.
3. Add chopped onion and cook for 3-4 minutes until tender, stirring often. Add garlic and cook for 1 minute.
4. Stir in the ground beef and herbs and cook for 5 minutes.
5. Pour in the marinara sauce and simmer for 5 minutes, stirring occasionally.
6. Remove the skillet from the heat and set ⅔ the meat sauce aside.
7. Cover the sauce with half of the broken noodles, then half of the cottage cheese, and one-third of the cheese. Then repeat the process with the same layers. Top with the remaining sauce and cheese.
8. Cover with a lid or foil and bake for 30 minutes.
9. Let it rest for 7-8 minutes before serving. Garnish with fresh parsley.

NUTRITIONAL INFO (PER SERVING):

Calories 868, Total Fat 24.3 g, Saturated Fat 7.1 g, Chol: 1562 mg, Sodium 1095 mg, Total Carbs: 96.2 g, Dietary Fiber 5.4 g, Total Sugars 16.5 g, Protein 63.8 g, Calcium 119 mg, Iron 24 mg, Potassium 1177 mg

Meat Extravaganza

GARLIC BUTTER STEAK

I don't even have to struggle to name a dish that everyone, or almost everyone, likes. It is definitely juicy steak with a brownish-golden crust. And a cast-iron skillet is the dish that makes the best steaks. Of course, it doesn't solve the smoke issue, even if you use a lid. The only thing that helps here is grilling outdoors.

The recipe is very simple and complex at the same time. Every detail is important, from patting the meat dry to heating the pan. I'm sharing my favorite recipe featuring butter and garlic, which has been tested and approved dozens of times.

3   5 minutes   20 minutes

INGREDIENTS:

- 3 sirloin/rib-eye/flat iron beef steaks (1-1½-inch (2.5-3.8 cm) thickness), at room temperature
- 1 Tbsp. avocado oil
- 2 Tbsp. unsalted butter

- 3 garlic cloves, crushed
- Fresh rosemary / thyme
- Coarse salt and pepper, to taste

HOW TO COOK:

1. Heat avocado oil in a cast-iron pan over medium heat for 5 minutes.
2. Pat the steaks dry and season with salt and pepper.
3. Add steaks to the preheated pan and cook for 4 minutes on each side until brown crusts form.
4. Set heat to low and add unsalted butter, crushed garlic, and herbs.
5. Continue cooking steaks, basting them with melted garlic butter from time to time. Check for the desired doneness with an instant-read thermometer:
6. medium-rare – 125^{0}F (50^{0}C)
7. medium well – 145^{0}F (65^{0}C)
8. Remove from the heat and let stand for 5-6 minutes before serving.
9. Slice and serve drizzled with garlic herb butter from the pan.

NUTRITIONAL INFO (PER SERVING):

Calories 200, Total Fat 12.6 g, Saturated Fat 6.7 g, Chol: 79 mg, Sodium 98 mg, Total Carbs: 1.3 g, Dietary Fiber 0.4 g, Total Sugars 0.1 g, Protein 20.2 g, Calcium 9 mg, Iron 12 mg, Potassium 292 mg

Meat Extravaganza

MEATBALLS IN TOMATO SAUCE

Juicy meatballs are a delicious, versatile dish for any occasion. If you think that meat is the main ingredient here and that you should focus on finding the right combination, you are only partly correct. I share the meatball recipe with marinara sauce, but you can get an entirely different dish by replacing the tomato sauce with creamy béchamel, garlic butter, cheese, or vegetable sauce.

It is easy to make and expands your daily menu with bright flavors.

6 15 minutes 45 minutes

INGREDIENTS:

FOR THE MEATBALLS:

- 1 lb. (450 g) ground beef
- 1 lb. (450 g) ground pork
- ½ cup (125 g) ricotta
- 1½ cups (180 g) breadcrumbs
- 2 whole eggs, slightly beaten
- ½ cup (30 g) grated Parmesan, divided
- ⅓ cup (80 ml) whole milk
- 2 Tbsp. fresh parsley, chopped
- 2 Tbsp. fresh thyme, chopped
- 3 garlic cloves, minced
- Salt and pepper, to taste
- 2 Tbsp. olive oil, for roasting

FOR THE SAUCE:

- 2 cans (28 oz. (800 g) each) crushed tomatoes
- 2 garlic cloves, minced
- ¼ tsp. smoked paprika
- 1 yellow onion (70 g), chopped
- 1 Tbsp. fresh basil, chopped
- 1 tsp. Italian seasoning
- Salt and pepper, to taste

HOW TO COOK:

1. Preheat the oven to 375⁰F (190⁰C).
2. Add all the ingredients for the meatballs to a bowl and mix until well combined.
3. Form uniform meatballs and arrange them in a greased cast-iron pan.
4. Bake them for 35 minutes until golden brown.
5. Meanwhile, combine all the ingredients for the tomato sauce.
6. Once the meatballs are cooked, remove the pan from the oven and cover the meatballs with tomato sauce. Simmer over low heat for 6-8 minutes.
7. Serve with your favorite spaghetti sprinkled with grated cheese and chopped parsley.

NUTRITIONAL INFO (PER SERVING):

Calories 662, Total Fat 21.6 g, Saturated Fat 7.7 g, Chol: 195 mg, Sodium 1090 mg, Total Carbs: 59.1 g, Dietary Fiber 10.4 g, Total Sugars 3.5 g, Protein 63.2 g, Calcium 446 mg, Iron 24 mg, Potassium 2158 mg

Meat Extravaganza

ROASTED LAMB CHOPS

This breaded lamb has everything you love: ease of preparation, ethereal flavor, and sophistication, making it the perfect weekend dinner or holiday treat. When we get together with friends, it's easier for me to make one or two racks of lamb for everyone and just slice it up. It's worth serving on the best platter with a beautiful tablecloth.

Coating the meat in the breadcrumb mixture helps this lamb of rack stay juicy.

4   15 minutes   30 minutes

- 1 (7-8 bones) (1½ - 2 lb./675-900 g) rack of lamb, trimmed and frenched
- ½ cup (60 g) breadcrumbs
- 2 garlic cloves, minced
- ⅓ cup (20 g) fresh rosemary / thyme / mint, chopped

- 1 Tbsp. Dijon mustard
- 1 Tbsp. lemon juice
- ½ tsp. salt, divided
- 1 tsp. black pepper, divided
- 4 Tsp. olive oil, divided

HOW TO COOK:

1. Preheat the oven to 450°F (230°C).
2. Mix breadcrumbs, 2 tablespoons of olive oil, minced garlic, chopped rosemary, ¼ teaspoon of salt, and ¼ teaspoon of black pepper in a small bowl.
3. Season the rack of lamb with the remaining salt and pepper.
4. Heat 2 tablespoons olive oil in a 12-inch (30 cm) cast-iron skillet over high heat. Sear the rack of lamb on each side until golden brown.
5. Remove the lamb from the skillet and coat it evenly with the breadcrumb mixture.
6. Return the breaded rack of lamb to the skillet and bake for 12-25 minutes, depending on the desired doneness.
7. Let stand for 8-10 minutes before carving.
8. Transfer to a platter and serve with roasted baby potatoes.

NUTRITIONAL INFO (PER SERVING):

Calories 402, Total Fat 21.6 g, Saturated Fat 6.5 g, Chol: 112 mg, Sodium 267 mg, Total Carbs: 14.1 g, Dietary Fiber 3.1 g, Total Sugars 1 g, Protein 36.9 g, Calcium 126 mg, Iron 5 mg, Potassium 97 mg

Meat Extravaganza

PORK CHOPS WITH MUSHROOMS

No matter how well you cook the meat, you will always face the sauce question. Even crispy pieces with juicy flesh seem incomplete without a spicy or tangy drizzle. You won't have that problem with this dish. What could be better than a buttery mushroom sauce with the sourness of red wine?

You won't want to waste a drop of this smooth sauce. Serve with your favorite neutral-tasting garnish to soak it all up.

2   7 minutes   15 minutes

INGREDIENTS:

- 2 pork chops (¾-inch (2 cm) thick), bone-in (at room temperature)
- 2 garlic cloves, crushed
- 1 garlic clove, diced
- 8 oz. (225 g) button mushrooms, diced
- ½ cup (120 ml) dry red wine
- ½ cup (120 ml) water
- 10 sprigs of thyme / rosemary
- 2 Tbsp. unsalted butter
- 1 Tbsp. olive oil
- Salt and pepper, to taste

HOW TO COOK:

1. Pat the pork chops dry and rub with crushed garlic, salt, and pepper.
2. Heat olive oil in a cast-iron skillet over medium heat. Add garlic and thyme sprigs and cook for 1-2 minutes, stirring occasionally.
3. Add 1 tablespoon of butter and diced mushrooms. Cook for 4-5 minutes until golden.
4. Remove mushrooms, thyme, and garlic from the skillet and set aside.
5. Melt the remaining butter in the skillet and add pork chops. Sear for 1 minute on each side until golden.
6. Return mushrooms and garlic to the skillet. Add red wine and water. Simmer for 5 minutes, flipping the chops once.
7. Remove from the heat, cover with a lid, and let rest for 5-7 minutes.
8. Serve with boiled potatoes and fresh seasonal salad. Drizzle the pork chops with the wine-mushroom sauce from the skillet.

NUTRITIONAL INFO (PER SERVING):

Calories 503, Total Fat 38.8 g, Saturated Fat 15.7 g, Chol: 99 mg, Sodium 148 mg, Total Carbs: 7.8 g, Dietary Fiber 1.8 g, Total Sugars 2.5 g, Protein 22.2 g, Calcium 56 mg, Iron 5 mg, Potassium 741 mg

CHILI CON CARNE

If you think of chili con carne, it's always about the spiciness. Of course, you can adjust the heat or add new flavors, but you will not even cook it if you are in the mood for something delicate. Chipotle pepper is the magic ingredient that turns ordinary meat with vegetables into this special dish.

I share the traditional recipe that starts with simmering the ingredients on the stovetop and finishes in the oven. But when I am too busy, I just combine all ingredients in a Dutch oven and pop it into a preheated oven for 1–2 hours, stirring occasionally. Let me tell you, that's pretty good, too.

| 6 | 15 minutes | 1⅓ hours |

INGREDIENTS:

- 2 lb. (900 g) ground beef
- 5 oz. (140 g) canned chipotle peppers
- 1 cup kidney beans (180 g), cooked / canned
- 1 white onion (70 g), diced
- 1 bell pepper (140 g). chopped
- 2 garlic cloves, minced

- 28 oz. (800 g) canned tomatoes, crushed
- 4 Tbsp. tomato paste
- 1 Tbsp. cacao powder
- 2 Tbsp. cumin powder
- 2 Tbsp. fresh parsley, chopped
- Salt and pepper, to taste

HOW TO COOK:

1. Preheat your oven to 375°F (190°C).
2. Heat 1 tablespoon of olive oil in a Dutch oven/large cast-iron pan over medium heat.
3. Add onions, garlic, and bell peppers and simmer for 3-4 minutes until tender, stirring occasionally.
4. Add ground beef, season with salt and pepper, and cook for 6-8 minutes, stirring occasionally.
5. Stir in canned tomatoes, kidney beans, tomato paste, chipotle peppers, cocoa, cumin, and chopped parsley. Sauté for 5-6 minutes, stirring occasionally.
6. Cover the Dutch oven with a lid and place in the oven. Cook for 1 hour.
7. Let rest for 20 minutes before serving.
8. Serve on a bed of rice and sprinkle with chopped fresh parsley.

NUTRITIONAL INFO (PER SERVING):

Calories 449, Total Fat 10.6 g, Saturated Fat 3.7 g, Chol: 134 mg, Sodium 127 mg, Total Carbs: 33.2 g, Dietary Fiber 8.2 g, Total Sugars 8.5 g, Protein 55.2 g, Calcium 78 mg, Iron 33 mg, Potassium 1636 mg

Meat Extravaganza

Baking Bonanza

CORNBREAD

I remember the taste of cornbread from my childhood. My mother made it dozens of times, and it is called comfort food. Even now, if I come across a recipe for perfectly moist bread with a crisp crust, I am sure to grab it. This recipe will work for you without fail.

You can upgrade it by adding grated Cheddar or chopped jalapeno. If you like the tangy flavor of honey, feel free to replace the white sugar with brown sugar or honey.

Cornbread goes well with chili, meat stew, grilled chicken, or soup.

6   10 minutes   25 minutes

- 1¼ cup (200 g) coarse cornmeal
- ¾ cup (100 g) all-purpose flour
- ⅓ cup (80 ml) whole milk
- 1 cup (240 ml) buttermilk / sour cream
- 2 Tbsp. white sugar/brown sugar / honey

- ½ tsp. salt
- 1 Tbsp. baking powder
- ½ tsp. baking soda
- 2 medium eggs, slightly beaten
- ½ cup (120 ml) unsalted butter, melted (divided)

HOW TO COOK:

1. Heat a 9-inch (23 cm) cast-iron skillet in a preheated 375°F (190°C) oven.

2. Mix all the dry ingredients in a bowl. Add the wet ingredients (except 1 tablespoon of the melted butter) and whisk together.

3. Take the skillet out from the oven and grease it with melted butter.

4. Pour the batter into the hot skillet and bake for 20-25 minutes. Use a toothpick to check for doneness.

5. Let it cool for 15 minutes and serve with salsa verde.

NUTRITIONAL INFO (PER SERVING):

Calories 463, Total Fat 19.6 g, Saturated Fat 11 g, Chol: 99 mg, Sodium 305 mg, Total Carbs: 63.6 g, Dietary Fiber 4.4 g, Total Sugars 7.5 g, Protein 10.2 g, Calcium 190 mg, Iron 3 mg, Potassium 537 mg

CHEESY GARLIC ROLLS

Frozen dinner buns make this recipe a breeze, but you can also knead your yeast dough and form small rolls. I was short of time and used my steady supply of frozen roll dough from the freezer. I just thawed them for some time before cooking.

You can make these garlic buns in two ways: cheesy or just garlic. Both options are tender, garlic-flavored, and buttery. Garlic buns pair perfectly with soups; cheesy ones are a great side dish or appetizer with different dips.

20 rolls   9 minutes   30 minutes
        (plus 2 hours to defrost)

- 20 Rhodes dinner rolls (or any homemade yeast buns)

- ½ cup (120 ml) unsalted butter, melted

- 5 garlic cloves, peeled and minced

- 2 Tbsp. fresh parsley leaves, chopped

- 1 cup (200 g) mozzarella, shredded (optional)

- ½ cup (60 g) cheddar / Parmesan, grated (optional)

HOW TO COOK:

1. Lightly grease a 12-inch cast-iron pan. Arrange frozen Rhodes dinner rolls in the pan, let them defrost, and rise for 1½-2 hours.

2. Preheat the oven to 375⁰F (190⁰C).

3. For cheesy buns, sprinkle them with shredded cheese. Skip this step if you want just garlic butter buns.

4. Mix melted butter, chopped parsley, and minced garlic in a small bowl. Drizzle the buns well with the garlic butter mixture.

5. Bake for 25-30 minutes until golden brown or the cheese is bubbly.

6. Let cool at room

NUTRITIONAL INFO (PER SERVING):

Calories 151, Total Fat 6.6 g, Saturated Fat 3.2 g, Chol: 14 mg, Sodium 189 mg, Total Carbs: 19.4 g, Dietary Fiber 0.5 g, Total Sugars 2 g, Protein 3.2 g, Calcium 16 mg, Iron 1 mg, Potassium 8 mg

APPLE PIE

Traditional apple pie is an easy recipe for beginners to learn how to bake. You can simplify the process by using canned apple pie filling. It always turns out great and inspires further culinary endeavors.

Use parchment paper for easier pie removal if you have an old cast-iron pan. Over time, you may want to experiment and add some berry filling to the apples. Anyway, apple pie is sure to become your go-to quick dessert.

6   15 minutes   50 minutes

INGREDIENTS:

- ½ cup (120 g) unsalted butter, divided
- ½ cup (120 g) light brown sugar
- 2 refrigerated 9-inch (23 cm) pie crusts

- 5 medium apples (Gala / Granny Smith / Honeycrisp / Golden Delicious), peeled and sliced
- ¾ cup (180 g) white sugar
- 1 tsp. ground cinnamon
- 1 tsp. cinnamon sugar

HOW TO COOK:

1. Preheat oven to 350°F (175°C). Melt ⅓ cup of the butter in the 9-inch (23 cm) cast-iron skillet.

2. Add brown sugar to the melted butter and cook for 2 minutes over medium-low heat until bubbling, stirring occasionally.

3. Remove from heat. Place a piecrust on the bubbling sugar in the skillet. Arrange apple slices on the crust. Sprinkle with ground cinnamon and white sugar.

4. Cover the apple filling with the second crust, crimping the edges of the crusts together. Make holes in the top crust to release steam. Brush the top crust with the remaining melted butter. Sprinkle with cinnamon sugar.

5. Bake for 30-40 minutes until golden brown.

6. Serve with a scoop of vanilla ice cream or whipped cream.

NUTRITIONAL INFO (PER SERVING):

Calories 459, Total Fat 17.6 g, Saturated Fat 10.7 g, Chol: 44 mg, Sodium 146 mg, Total Carbs: 79.1 g, Dietary Fiber 4.7 g, Total Sugars 6915 g, Protein 1 g, Calcium 26 mg, Iron 1 mg, Potassium 232 mg

HOMEMADE BREAD

The coziest way to have fresh fragrant bread at home is to bake it in the Dutch oven. It produces a crispy golden crust and a delicate crumb. You can use your bread machine for no-fuss kneading and bake the loaf in the oven. This is a perfect method for newbies to start their baking journey with a Dutch oven.

I suggest a basic white bread recipe for baking in a cast-iron pot, but you can experiment by adding herbs, garlic powder, grated hard cheese, or seeds. The steps are the same. Be ready to adjust the amount of water and flour, a tablespoon at a time, to get the right texture and perfect rise.

8   20 minutes   45 minutes
          (plus 5 hours for rising)

- 4 cups (520 g) all-purpose flour
- 2 cups (480 ml) lukewarm water
- 1 Tbsp. olive oil
- 1 tsp. sea salt
- 2¼ tsp. (7 g) active dry yeast

HOW TO COOK:

1. Dissolve yeast in the water in a large bowl. Add salt.
2. Add flour and mix by hand until the dough is uniform and sticky. Adjust the amount of water and flour if the dough is too dry or too wet.
3. Coat the dough and let it rise in a warm place for 1½-2 hours until doubled in size.
4. Push down the dough with your hands several times, cover it again, and let it rise for 2 hours more.
5. Once the dough has doubled again, transfer it to a large piece of parchment paper dusted with flour. Form a ball using your oiled hands. Don't worry if the dough doesn't hold the shape, the Dutch oven will take care of that.
6. Meanwhile, preheat the oven to 450⁰F (230⁰C) and place the covered Dutch oven inside for 20 minutes.
7. Gently lift the dough onto the parchment paper and transfer it to the bowl. Let it rest and rise until the Dutch oven is ready.
8. Carefully remove the hot pot from the oven and transfer the dough in the parchment paper into the Dutch oven. Cover with a hot lid.
9. Bake for 30 minutes. Open the lid and bake for 10-20 minutes more until golden brown.
10. Remove the loaf with the parchment paper from the Dutch oven and let it cool on a rack for 20 minutes.
11. Slice and serve with herb butter or spicy meat stew.

NUTRITIONAL INFO (PER SERVING):

Calories 254, Total Fat 2.6 g, Saturated Fat 0.4 g, Chol: 0 mg, Sodium 236 mg, Total Carbs: 49.9 g, Dietary Fiber 1.9 g, Total Sugars 0.2 g, Protein 7.2 g, Calcium 10 mg, Iron 3 mg, Potassium 87 mg

CHICAGO-STYLE PIZZA

It seems that deep-dish pizza is made for our experimentation and use of leftovers. I have added sliced mushrooms, chopped onions, pepperoni, and diced olives — every time, it turned out great, and I was asked for a refill. Baking in cast iron makes crispy golden edges with a generous, juicy filling inside. If you don't have cornmeal at home, don't be in a hurry to give up on this recipe. Just skip this ingredient and go on cooking!

Try making your own pizza sauce by simmering juicy tomatoes with minced garlic, chopped red onions, olive oil, and some Italian herbs.

8   20 minutes   40 minutes
(plus 60 minutes for rising)

INGREDIENTS:

FOR THE DOUGH:

- 1½ cups (200 g) all-purpose flour
- ¾ cup (180 ml) lukewarm water
- ¼ cup (40 g) cornmeal
- 2 Tbsp. olive oil
- 1 Tbsp. liquid honey
- 1 Tbsp. active dry yeast

FOR THE TOPPING:

- 10 oz. (280 g) Mozzarella cheese, shredded
- 1 lb. (450 g) Italian sausages, cooked and crumbled
- ½ cup (30 g) Parmesan, shredded
- 2 cups (480 ml) pizza sauce

HOW TO COOK:

1. Dissolve yeast in lukewarm water in a large bowl.

2. Add flour, cornmeal, olive oil, and honey. Knead the dough using a mixer with a kneading hook or by hand. Transfer the dough to an oiled bowl, cover, and let it rise for 1 hour.

3. Meanwhile, preheat the oven to 425°F (220°C). Grease a 9-inch (23 cm) cast-iron pan with olive oil and dust with 1 tablespoon of cornmeal.

4. Transfer the dough to a floured surface and roll it into a 15-inch (38 cm) circle. Feel free to use more flour if it is sticky.

5. Transfer the rolled-out dough to the cast-iron pan and press lightly into the bottom and sides with your fingers.

6. Evenly spread the shredded Mozzarella and cooked sausage over the dough. Pour over pizza sauce and sprinkle shredded Parmesan on top.

7. Cook for 30-35 minutes until the crust is golden brown.

8. Remove from the oven and let it cool for 10 minutes before slicing and serving.

NUTRITIONAL INFO (PER SERVING):

Calories 492, Total Fat 29.2 g, Saturated Fat 11.4 g, Chol: 64 mg, Sodium 916 mg, Total Carbs: 33.6 g, Dietary Fiber 2.4 g, Total Sugars 4.5 g, Protein 23.8 g, Calcium 100 mg, Iron 3 mg, Potassium 216 mg

Delectable Desserts

BLUEBERRY COBBLER

Cobbler is an absolutely gorgeous and healthy dessert consisting of berries or fruits with a flaky biscuit top. It is like a cake but without a bottom crust. It's our favorite summer dessert. I've made cherry, plum, peach, and mixed cobblers, and I'm not going to stop experimenting.

The best accompaniment for a good old blueberry cobbler is a scoop of vanilla ice cream or a dollop of whipped cream. It adds a little creaminess to the sweet, syrupy berry dessert.

8 20 minutes 45 minutes

INGREDIENTS:

- 1 cup (130 g) all-purpose flour
- 1 tsp. baking powder
- ¼ tsp. sea salt
- ¼ tsp. baking soda
- ½ cup (120 g) unsalted butter
- 1½ (360 g) white sugar

- 1 tsp. lemon zest
- 1 cup (240 ml) whole milk
- 2 cups (350 g) fresh / frozen blueberries
- 1 tsp. ground cinnamon

HOW TO COOK:

1. Preheat the oven to 350⁰F (175⁰C).

2. Meanwhile, heat a 10-inch (25 cm) cast-iron skillet over low heat and melt the butter.

3. Add blueberries, lemon zest, and ½ cup of sugar. Cook for 3-4 minutes, stirring occasionally.

4. Combine flour, baking soda, baking powder, salt, the remaining sugar, and milk in a bowl. Mix until smooth.

5. Cover the blueberries with the batter and bake for 35-45 minutes until golden brown.

6. Remove it from the oven and let it cool for 10 minutes before serving.

NUTRITIONAL INFO (PER SERVING):

Calories 376, Total Fat 13.6 g, Saturated Fat 8.3 g, Chol: 35 mg, Sodium 138 mg, Total Carbs: 64.6 g, Dietary Fiber 1.4 g, Total Sugars 50.5 g, Protein 3.2 g, Calcium 71 mg, Iron 1 mg, Potassium 158 mg

Delectable Desserts

CHOCOLATE BROWNIES

This moist, gooey chocolate dessert originated in the United States in the late 19th century, but it has since supplanted many traditional chocolate cakes around the world. You can find British, Swedish, or Dutch brownies with their own names.

Every nuance matters when baking brownies — the type of butter, the flour, the bitterness of the chocolate chips, and even the baking dish. A cast-iron skillet ensures that the dough heats evenly and slowly and maintains the temperature over the entire surface. The dessert cooks quicker and continues to cook even after it's been removed from the oven, so take care to remove the brownies a little earlier than you would with a traditional brownie pan.

8   15 minutes   30 minutes

INGREDIENTS:

- 1 cup (130 g) all-purpose flour
- 1 cup (100 g) cocoa powder
- 1 cup (240 g) unsalted butter, melted
- ¾ cup (180 g) white sugar
- ¾ cup (180 g) brown sugar / jaggery powder

- 4 large eggs, at room temperature
- 2 tsp. vanilla extract
- ½ tsp. sea salt
- 1 cup (160 g) chocolate chips
- ½ cup (70 g) toasted walnuts / pecans, chopped

HOW TO COOK:

1. Preheat the oven to 350^0F (180^0C).

2. Combine melted butter with white and brown sugar in a large bowl.

3. Add eggs, vanilla extract, flour, cocoa powder, and salt. Lightly whisk the batter.

4. Add chocolate chips and walnuts and mix.

5. Pour the batter into a 10-inch (25 cm) cast-iron skillet. Sprinkle with some chocolate chips and walnuts.

6. Bake for 30 minutes, checking with a toothpick for doneness. Remove the skillet from the oven when the brownies are just set to the touch because the skillet will be hot for a long time, and the brownies will continue cooking.

7. Let them cool slightly before serving. Brownies pair perfectly with a scoop of vanilla ice cream.

NUTRITIONAL INFO (PER SERVING):

Calories 672, Total Fat 39.6 g, Saturated Fat 21.7 g, Chol: 162 mg, Sodium 233 mg, Total Carbs: 76.9 g, Dietary Fiber 5.4 g, Total Sugars 55.5 g, Protein 11 g, Calcium 99 mg, Iron 4 mg, Potassium 523 mg

Delectable Desserts

CHOCOLATE CHIP COOKIE

This chocolate chip cookie is the perfect treat for Valentine's Day, a children's party, or a chilly winter weekend. It has a chewy crumb, and a soft crust sprinkled with chocolate chips and coarse salt.

Catch a few tips for perfect results: make sure the sugar-butter mixture is slightly cool to not cook the beaten eggs. Also, stir the chocolate chips into the cooled batter and pour the batter into a cold skillet to avoid melting the chips. This cookie is a study in simplicity — it takes longer to write than to cook. Start making!

6	15 minutes	30 minutes

INGREDIENTS:

- 2½ cups (330 g) all-purpose flour
- 2 tsp. baking powder
- 1 tsp. baking soda
- ¼ tsp. sea salt
- 1 cup (240 ml) unsalted butter, melted
- 1 cup (240 g) light brown sugar

- ½ cup (120 g) white sugar
- 1 large egg, whisked
- 2 egg yolks, whisked
- 2 tsp. vanilla extract
- 10 oz. chocolate chips
- Coarse salt, for sprinkling

HOW TO COOK:

1. Preheat the oven to 350⁰F (180⁰C).
2. Mix all-purpose flour, baking powder, soda, and sea salt in a bowl.
3. Blend melted butter with white and brown sugar in another bowl. Add whisked eggs, yolks, and vanilla extract.
4. Combine dry and wet ingredients and mix until smooth. Add chocolate chips and stir in.
5. Pour the batter into a 12-inch (30 cm) cast-iron skillet and bake for 20-30 minutes, checking with a toothpick for doneness.
6. Sprinkle with some coarse salt and serve with vanilla ice cream.

NUTRITIONAL INFO (PER SERVING):

Calories 989, Total Fat 47.6 g, Saturated Fat 30.3 g, Chol: 194 mg, Sodium 496 mg, Total Carbs: 130 g, Dietary Fiber 3.1 g, Total Sugars 83.5 g, Protein 11.6 g, Calcium 224 mg, Iron 4 mg, Potassium 485 mg

Delectable Desserts

BANANA BREAD

Americans are big banana bread fans, eating it as a hearty snack, as a complement to morning coffee or tea, or as a dessert with frosting. This recipe is easy to put into action, even on busy nights. Very ripe bananas make it moist, and the nuts add protein, giving it a tangy flavor and aroma.

Making it in a cast-iron pan allows the banana bread to bake evenly. Such bread sometimes fails to cook all the way through the center in a regular bread pan, but this will never happen with a cast-iron skillet.

| 6 | 15 minutes | 50 minutes |

INGREDIENTS:

- 2 cups (260 g) all-purpose flour
- ½ cup (120 g) unsalted butter, softened
- ½ cup (120 g) light brown/white sugar
- A pinch of salt
- ⅛ tsp. nutmeg

- ¼ tsp. cinnamon
- 2 medium eggs
- 1 Tbsp. baking powder
- 3 large ripe bananas, mashed
- ¼ cup (60 ml) sour cream
- ½ cup (50 g) pecans / walnuts / chocolate chips

HOW TO COOK:

1. Preheat the oven to 350⁰F (180⁰C). Line a 10-inch (25 cm) cast-iron skillet with parchment paper.
2. Whisk the softened butter with brown sugar. Mix in the eggs, one at a time.
3. Add mashed bananas, sour cream, flour, and baking powder, and mix well.
4. Spread the batter in the skillet. Press pecans into the top.
5. Bake for 45-55 minutes, checking with a toothpick for doneness.
6. Let it cool completely before serving.

NUTRITIONAL INFO (PER SERVING):

Calories 537, Total Fat 25 g, Saturated Fat 12.6 g, Chol: 101 mg, Sodium 149 mg, Total Carbs: 71.2 g, Dietary Fiber 4 g, Total Sugars 28.5 g, Protein 8.2 g, Calcium 164 mg, Iron 3 mg, Potassium 640 mg

Delectable Desserts

FROM THE AUTHOR

My name is Christopher Lester, and I've always been drawn to the culinary arts. From an early age, **I liked the magic that happens in the kitchen,** where simple ingredients are transformed into extraordinary dishes. Over the years, I have honed my skills and acquired unique techniques, becoming a renowned culinary wizard and flavor magician.

My journey began with a thirst for knowledge and a desire to learn from the best. I sought out the biggest names in the culinary realm to soak up their wisdom. From celebrity chefs to seasoned culinary experts, I was like a sponge, soaking up their expertise and incorporating it into my repertoire.

But my world didn't just revolve around the kitchen. I had two beautiful daughters who brought joy and laughter into my life. When I wasn't enchanting the culinary world with my creations, I was spending time with them and my faithful companion in the kitchen, Jack, our beloved family dog. Together we would go on adventures, explore the wonders of nature, and share precious moments.

In my free time, I loved to put on my worn apron, a symbol of my culinary prowess, and invite friends and family to gather around the table. The joy of creating festive dishes for my loved ones was incomparable. **Tantalizing aromas filled the air, heralding the beginning of the culinary feast.**

OUR RECOMMENDATIONS

Dutch Oven Cookbook:
Easy-to-Follow Delicious Recipes
for One-Pot Meals

Bread Machine & Oven Cookbook:
Delicious Recipes for Homemade
Bread, Cakes, Buns, Bagels,
Cookies, Pies

Copyright

Manufactured by Amazon.ca
Bolton, ON

36094521R00061